KINGFISHER KINGPINS

The Superbook of
BATTLES

Brian Williams

KINGFISHER BOOKS

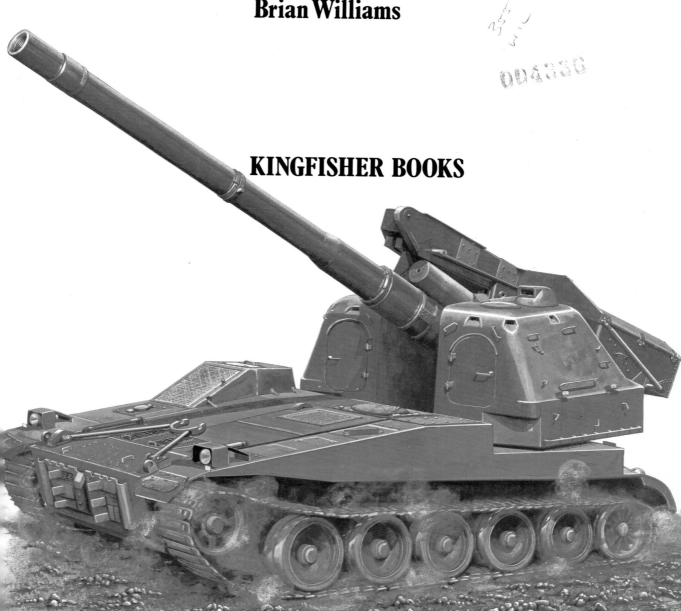

Contents

This revised edition published in 1985 by Kingfisher Books Limited
Elsley Court, 20–22 Great Titchfield Street, London W1P 7AD
A Grisewood & Dempsey Company
Originally published in hardcover by Ward Lock Limited in 1981
in the *Wonder Book* series.

BRITISH LIBRARY CATALOGUING IN PUBLICATION DATA
Williams, Brian, *1943–*
    Battles. – 2nd ed. – (Kingpins)
    1. Battles – Juvenile literature 2. Military history – Juvenile literature
I. Title   II. Williams, Brian, *1943–*
    Wonder book of battles
    904'.7   D25

ISBN 0-86272-178-4

Edited by Angela Royston
Designed by Keith Groom
Cover design by the Pinpoint Design Company
Printed in Hong Kong by the South China Printing Co.

Cover: An 8-wheeled German Panzer tank.
Previous page: A modern Swedish self-propelled gun.

Battles

War and battles are as old as man. Several factors may decide the outcome of a battle. Luck, for example: when King Harold was killed by a stray Norman arrow at the Battle of Hastings, his hard-pressed army broke in despair, and history was made. It has been said too that the most successful general is the one with the largest army. But this is not always so, and many famous victories have been won against apparently overwhelming odds.

This book looks at some famous battles—on land, sea and in the air. Each has its own story: of skilful tactics, careful planning, surprise and concealment, grim defence and dashing attack, and very often of muddle and confusion too. The invention of new weapons has helped to win battles, and the arms race has actually been going on for hundreds of years. But more than anything, the story of battle is about courage and determination—the soldier's will to win.

Knight jousting at a tournament

Warriors Long Ago

In the heat of battle, many factors can affect the outcome—the skill of a commander, the bravery of his soldiers, the kind of weapons they have, and so on. But time after time, the common soldier has held the key to victory.

The first soldiers were probably also skilful hunters; their weapons were rocks, spears, clubs and slingshots. It was in Mesopotamia, in the Middle East, that the first proper armies appeared. Even then, battles were little more than a series of fights between small groups of warriors, who gathered on the battlefield.

Some 3500 years ago, the Egyptians and Assyrians organized more effective armies. The Egyptians used horse-drawn chariots, and relied on speed to defeat their enemies. Around 1000 BC the Assyrian army was the most feared in the world. It used chariots, cavalry and infantry, and its soldiers were tough and well equipped.

In many respects the first 'professional' soldier was the Roman legionary. A legion was a regiment of 5000 men, and the men's discipline and training were so good that for 500 years the Roman army was seldom defeated. The legions fought in Europe,

The Assyrians, with their battering rams, scaling ladders and well-protected archers, were masters of siege warfare.

Battle

Africa and the Middle East, marching swiftly into battle along the excellent roads built by their military engineers.

Most Roman soldiers fought on foot, advancing on the enemy with shields and swords. Their main missiles were arrows which they fired and spears or javelins which they threw. Infantry made up the bulk of most armies until recent times. In the Middle Ages, poorly armed peasants were the 'rank and file' soldiers. The 'armoured corps' of medieval war were knights on horseback, protected by coats of mail and steel plate.

▼ The medieval knight fought on horseback. His chief weapons were the lance, sword, axe and mace. Chain mail was not strong enough to protect the wearer from arrows fired from crossbows, so it was gradually replaced by a complete suit of steel-plated armour.

The Roman legionary was armed with two throwing spears or javelins, a short stabbing sword and a shield. He was tough, well trained and versatile.

French armour 1200s

English armour 1300s

German armour early 1400s

The Warrior's Code

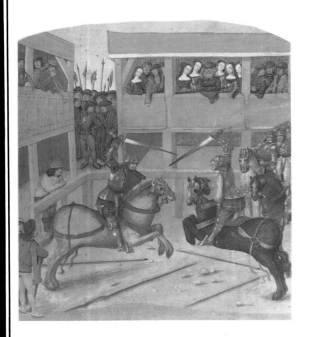

The warrior became a special kind of man, a hero in fact. Tales of brave deeds were very popular, and some religions even encouraged warriors to die in battle. The Vikings believed that dead heroes went to Valhalla to feast with the gods. The Arabs too believed that warriors who fell in battle went to Paradise. Such beliefs made men fearless and scornful of death.

Honour was important to the soldier. Among the Anglo-Saxons, a man was expected to fight and die for his lord. A quarrel between two warriors often led to a blood feud involving their families, friends and servants. Such loyalty gave rise to the important medieval idea of chivalry.

◀ **Knights fought mock battles or jousts, at tournaments.**

The Samurai

These warriors of medieval Japan would kill themselves rather than surrender. They fought on horseback and their favourite weapons were their long swords. Their elaborate and colourful armour protected them and intimidated their enemies. When firearms were introduced they despised them as 'cowards' weapons'.

The samurai formed a proud warrior caste, fanatically loyal to their warlord. Their downfall came, ironically, at the hands of humble foot-soldiers armed with muskets. Not even samurai armour could withstand powder and ball. The samurai's defeat showed that the day of the proud warrior-hero was coming to an end.

The samurai fought for the great warlords of Japan. At the battle of Nagashino in 1575 their wild charges were beaten off by ranks of musketeers.

A medieval knight was supposed to obey the rules of chivalry—to fight bravely in battle, but also show respect for the poor and weak. A boy of noble birth had to train long and hard before becoming a knight. To practise the skills of war, knights took part in mock battles and tournaments.

The rules of chivalry were usually obeyed on the real battlefield. If a knight was captured, he could expect fair treatment and a safe return home (after the payment of a ransom). A wound was far more dangerous than capture. For medical knowledge was so poor that if a wounded man escaped death on the battlefield he was almost certain to die in the clumsy hands of the surgeons.

▶ **A wounded soldier receives medical aid on the battlefield in 1528. Army surgeons were so unskilled that they were little more than butchers.**

Fighting men from three periods in history: left to right: a Swiss musketeer of 1673; an American soldier of the 6th South Carolina Regiment during the American War of Independence; and a French cavalryman of the Napoleonic era. At this time cavalry was the pride of most armies.

Professional Soldiers

New weapons produced a new kind of soldier. He was better trained and better armed than the foot-soldiers of the Middle Ages (who often went to war armed only with pitch-forks and clubs). Gone too were the ponderous armoured knights on their heavy horses. By the 1700s only cavalry wore any form of body armour.

Uniforms were slow to develop. At first most regiments were named after the nobles who formed and often led them. When there was no war, the officers went off to hunt while the men returned to their farms. So most troops marched into battle with very little training. Discipline was brutal and pay and food were poor.

During the 1700s, small armies of professional soldiers became common. They wore the brightly coloured uniforms of their regiments and armies.

A battle was a confusion of smoke and noise. Commanders seldom had a clear view of what was going on. Troops practised formal drilling, and marched into line in full view of the enemy before a battle began. Artillery fire was still too slow and inaccurate to do much damage.

In the 1800s weapons became more deadly and armies began to change. Pay, conditions and training improved slowly. Brightly coloured uniforms (too easily spotted by snipers) gave way to dull khaki and grey. Most armies remained small until the outbreak of World War I in 1914. Then millions of men were called up to join the fighting.

▲ In 1914, shortly after the outbreak of World War I, the Allied armies halted the German advance at the battle of the Marne. Losses on both sides were huge. The armies dug themselves into trenches, and a new terrible kind of warfare had begun.

▲ During the French Revolution, the French army became a confused mixture of regular troops and raw recruits. However, patriotic fervour inspired the French to victories over the Austrians and Prussians. At the battle of Fleurus in 1794 they even tried using a hot air balloon as an observation post.

▶ Although modern weapons make mass destruction possible, the soldier remains a key factor. Guerillas, living off the land, can win against much superior forces—as was shown in Vietnam. Here the modern weaponry of the Americans could not beat a seldom-seen enemy.

Conquering the World

Saladin (1138–1193) led the armies of Islam against the Crusaders. He made himself master of Egypt and Syria and in 1187 captured Jerusalem from the Christians. Not even Richard the Lionheart could wrest the Holy Land from him.

A few remarkable soldiers have made history on the battlefield. Their skill as leaders created empires, and with each victory their fame grew. Hannibal, the great Carthaginian general, was for years Rome's most dangerous foe. Saladin defeated the Crusaders in Palestine, and Genghis Khan ruled the vast Mongol Empire, but most famous of all was Alexander the Great.

In 334 BC Alexander, aged 22, led the Greeks against the might of the Persian Empire. At Gaugamela, in Syria in 331 BC, he defeated a huge Persian army led by King Darius. The Greek phalanxes calmly drew the Persians away from their specially prepared ground. When charged by chariots, the Greeks opened ranks, allowing the

▼ This mosaic, found in the ruins of Pompeii, shows the Battle of Issus in 333 BC. The Persian king Darius flees in his chariot as Alexander (left) approaches on horseback.

Generals

Persians to rush through to be attacked and destroyed by the strong Greek rearguard. Before the dismayed Persians could attack again, Alexander led his crack cavalry into their midst. Darius himself was forced to flee, and, at this, the entire Persian army broke and ran.

Alexander never lost an important battle. He led his army as far as India, and there he wept to find there were 'no new worlds to conquer'.

Genghis Khan

Genghis Khan (1167-1227) was probably the most feared conqueror of all time. His armies swept out of the East as far as Russia. To his victims, who had no idea who the Mongols were, it seemed as if they were being punished by Heaven. They called Genghis the 'Wrath of God'

The Roman general Scipio with fresh troops and new tactics finally defeated Hannibal. At Zama, south of Carthage, Hannibal lost his last great battle in 202 BC. His war elephants panicked when the Romans blew trumpets and scattered metal spikes in their path.

◄ Gustavus Adolphus became king of Sweden in 1611. His troops wore uniforms and his officers had maps (modern ideas for the time). His army was well treated and responded with loyalty and fighting spirit.

Below left: Frederick the Great was a firm but fair ruler. He inherited a strong army from his father and improved its training and discipline until it was the best fighting force in Europe.

▼ Napoleon's genius lay in doing the right thing at the right time. At Austerlitz he knew he must fight, and win, before winter set in. Boldness, timing and the skill of his marshals won him a great victory.

Frederick the Great

Masters of War

Until the 18th century kings often led their armies into battle. Gustavus Adolphus, king of Sweden (1594–1632), organized the most up-to-date army of his age. His musketeers and pikemen fought side by side, protecting each other. They formed up with small cavalry units to make a chessboard pattern. The Swedes' speedy attacks surprised the slow-moving infantry squares of the Catholic League, whom Gustavus defeated at the Battle of Breitenfeld in 1631, shown in the photo on the left.

England's greatest general was the Duke of Marlborough. At Blenheim in 1704, Marlborough and Prince Eugene of Austria defeated the French and Bavarians. First they attacked on the flanks. When the enemy moved troops from his centre to meet these attacks, Marlborough's artillery bombarded the weakened positions and then his cavalry smashed through the centre of the enemy lines to complete the victory.

Frederick the Great, the warrior-king of Prussia, believed in strict discipline and hard training. During the Seven Years War, the Prussians faced the combined armies of France, Austria and Russia. Yet by fast marching and skilful use of light cannon, they won victory after victory. Frederick's example was admired by an even greater general, Napoleon.

Napoleon had the knack of choosing the right moment to attack. His greatest triumph was at Austerlitz in 1805, when he defeated a larger Russian and Austrian army. By pretending to retreat, Napoleon tempted the enemy to give up a good position on high ground. He stormed their lines with infantry, divided their forces and then turned his cannon on them.

Napoleon Bonaparte

War

The Greek phalanx was a formation which made the most of infantry as a 'shock weapon'. Ranks of warriors advanced side by side, presenting a wall of shields and spear points to the enemy. If one man fell, another quickly took his place.

The crossbow was loaded by means of a ratchet device. It fired a metal bolt which could pierce armour at 100 metres (110 yards). Crossbows were so deadly that for a time the Pope outlawed their use against all but heathens. However the crossbow was challenged by the longbow. This had a much longer range, up to 250 metres (270 yards), and could fire 16 arrows a minute compared with only two or three by the crossbow. Such weapons gave the humble foot soldier more than a fighting chance against armoured knights. If his horse were killed, a knight on foot, weighed down by his armour, was an easy victim.

Crossbow

Longbow

Machines

The Arms Race

A well-trained soldier is the basic 'war machine'. New weapons give him an added advantage—surprise. The Greeks and Romans did not invent new weapons, but they surprised their enemies by adopting new tactics—fighting in close formation, for example.

The 'arms race' for the possession of 'super-weapons' is nothing new. During the Middle Ages, archers argued the merits of the crossbow and longbow. Both were good weapons, and a match even for the armoured knights who were the 'tanks' of the medieval battlefield.

Gunpowder, and the development of muskets and cannon, changed the way battles were fought. Castle walls could not withstand gunfire. Generals were at first slow to see that firearms were the weapons of the future, and that mechanical war was being made possible by science.

The Testudo

The testudo or 'tortoise' was a formation used by Roman soldiers when advancing against enemy fire. Each man raised his shield above his head, locking it against the edges of the shields on either side. The result was an armoured 'shell' for protection against arrows, spears, rocks and even boiling water. The testudo was a tribute to the Romans' training and discipline, for it must have needed great courage to move forward in this way against a fort manned by barbarian warriors.

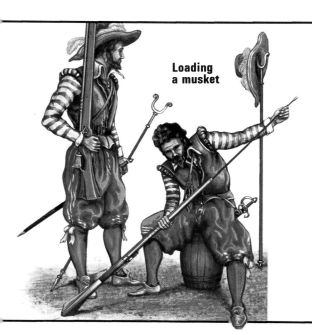

Loading a musket

Gustavus, the 'father of modern warfare', introduced wheel-lock muskets and light cannon.

Swedish cannon, about 1630

Attack and Defence

Every new weapon meets its match, for **sooner** or later attack is countered by **defence**. Long before gunpowder was **known**, the Romans used artillery in the **shape** of giant catapults and crossbows to **attack** forts. The ancient world also had a mysterious and deadly flame-throwing weapon, known as 'Greek fire'.

Similar siege engines were used in the Middle Ages to bombard castles, and were probably just as effective as the early cannon. The attackers used scaling ladders and towers to climb over the walls, and dug tunnels under them. A siege might last many months until hunger or sickness forced the defenders to give in. Cannon were frightening and noisy weapons, but they were not accurate or powerful enough to win battles on their own until the 1800s. Then the heavy losses suffered by both sides during the American Civil War showed that troops could no longer advance in the open against quick-firing guns.

However, this lesson was not fully learned until World War I. Unable to advance, whole armies took refuge in trenches. Battles were fought and thousands of soldiers died over a few metres of muddy ground, turned into a wasteland by exploding artillery shells.

Above left: A castle under siege during the Middle Ages. Soldiers are using siege towers and ladders to try and climb over the walls, whilst giant catapults and bombards (early cannon) hurl stones to breach the defences.

▲ A print showing the Duke of Wellington entering Salamanca in Spain during the Peninsular War. In the early 1800s cavalry (dragoons, hussars, lancers and so on) were the most mobile and dashing units.

▶ Canadian infantry defending their trenches against attack at Ypres in 1915. In the bloody fighting of World War I frontal attacks were terribly costly and seldom successful.

Mechanical Warfare

Rapid Fire

This Gatling gun, first used during the American Civil War, had as many as ten barrels which fired in succession as a handle was cranked. The even more deadly Maxim gun of 1884 was the first truly automatic lightweight machine gun. Such weapons were a far cry from the first hand guns, crude cannon mounted on wooden shafts.

The Italian genius Leonardo da Vinci sketched war machines and even aircraft in the early 1500s. But such ideas remained only dreams until the 1800s and the dawn of the machine age.

Steam power foreshadowed the end of the great sailing warship, although navies were slow to change. The first naval battle between ironclad steam ships took place during the American Civil War, but the first really 'modern' battleship, HMS *Dreadnought*, did not appear until 1906.

Few people thought that aircraft would have any fighting role in war, but during World War I fighter and bomber planes played a growing part. The tank, crawling on caterpillar tracks, also fought in the 1914–1918 War. In the 1940s aircraft and tanks combined in the German 'Blitzkrieg' attacks which swept across Europe.

▼ The *Holland* (1898) was the first truly seaworthy submarine. Built in the USA it had petrol engines for surface cruising and electric motors for use under water (like most of its successors).

▲ The first naval battle between ironclads was in 1862 during the American Civil War. *Merrimack* was a wooden frigate converted by the South into an armoured ram with ten guns. The North's *Monitor* had two guns mounted in a revolving turret. This duel at sea was indecisive, but showed the shape of things to come.

▶ An aerial 'dogfight' between biplanes in World War I. At first, generals could see little use for aircraft (save for spying) and warplanes did not even carry guns. Later, fighter 'aces' became national heroes.

Science Goes to War	
Gunpowder rockets in China	before 1000
First cannon used in Europe	early 1300s
Matchlock musket in use	by 1500s
Improved flintlock musket	early 1600s
Breech-loading needle gun	1827
Colt revolver	1836
Rifle (range 200 m, 220 yd)	1850
Armoured warship	1859
Gatling gun	1863
Maxim machine gun	1884
Holland submarine	1898
Lee Enfield rifle (range 2000 m, 2200 yd)	1902
Dreadnought battleship	1906
First use of tanks	1916
Jet aircraft (He. 178)	1939
Guided missile (V2)	1944
Atomic bomb	1945

▼ Tanks were first used in World War I, but did not come into their own until World War II. More than 1500 tanks took part in the desert battle of Alamein (1942), where conditions were ideal for armoured warfare.

The Will

The will to win is a mysterious quality. It explains why David killed Goliath, why Henry V won at Agincourt and why Nelson won at Trafalgar. Great men can inspire their followers to heroism and triumph against apparently overwhelming odds.

Of all the Ancient Greek heroes, one of the most celebrated was Pheidippides, a famous athlete. When the Persians were invading in 490 BC, he ran 240 kilometres (150 miles) to fetch help, fought in the battle of Marathon, and then, without rest, ran to Athens with the first news of the Greek victory. Having gasped his message, he fell dead. But his deed is remembered in the modern marathon race.

Time and again, soldiers have succeeded in turning seemingly inevitable defeat into victory. Weight of numbers does not always guarantee success.

to Win

Against All Odds

Salamis

This historic sea battle was fought in 480 BC during the wars between the Greeks and Persians. The mighty Persian fleet of up to 1000 galleys sailed into the narrow strait near the island of Salamis. The Greeks, with some 380 ships, retreated, drawing the Persians after them. Then the Greeks attacked, trying to ram the Persians who, hemmed in by sheer numbers, had no room to turn. In the confusion 200 Persian ships were sunk or captured. The rest fled and never challenged the Greek navy again.

At the Battle of Crecy, the English were led by Edward III and his son, the Black Prince. The victory was won by the skill of the English archers and the greater discipline among the English ranks.

Famous Victories

During the Hundred Years War, English armies won three famous victories over the French: at Crecy (1346), Poitiers (1356) and Agincourt (1415). Each time the English, outnumbered, took up a good defensive position. Their archers' longbows outshot the French crossbows in range and speed of fire. The French bowmen, unable to get close enough to shoot, only got in the way of their knights who were trying to charge the English lines. At Agincourt the weather also helped the English. Heavy rain turned the ground into a quagmire, and many of the heavily armoured French men-at-arms were trampled to death.

Freedom Fighters

▲ Yorktown 1781 and the British finally surrender to the American rebels. The American War of Independence, begun in 1775, was over. Another 100 years and more were to pass before Canada, Australia, India and the rest of the British Empire became independent too.

▼ Simon Bolivar marched against the Spanish in 1819 with no more than 2500 men. Many died crossing the Andes, but their arrival in New Granada took the Spanish completely by surprise. Bolivar's army won the Battle of Boyaca and entered Bogota in triumph.

Every country has its national heroes, who have fought for freedom when their country was under foreign rule. In the 11th century Rodrigo Diaz (El Cid) fought for Spain against the invading Moors. In France, Joan of Arc was executed in 1431 for her attempts to free her country from English rule. In Switzerland, William Tell inspired his countrymen to oppose the tyrannous Austrian rule.

Some people have become symbols for freedom even beyond their own country. George Washington, who led the American fight for independence from the British, inspired many others. South America was liberated from Spanish rule by two brilliant leaders, Jose de San Martin and Simon Bolivar, who gave his name to the country of Bolivia.

Most freedom fighters use guerilla tactics. Small groups, often working independently, ambush and sabotage the occupying force. Garibaldi was the greatest guerilla fighter of the 1800s, leading the struggle for Italian freedom from the Spanish and Austrians. During World War II, resistance groups fought the German occupation all over Europe.

In recent years many former colonies have gained independence from their European rulers. Some have had to fight to achieve it. In Vietnam, the French were finally driven out by the cunning of Vo Nguyen Giap. Guerilla armies fought in Angola and Mozambique against their Portuguese rulers. In 1979, after years of fighting, the minority white government in Rhodesia gave way to black majority rule.

In 1954 the French tried to lure the Viet Minh guerillas, led by General Giap, into a pitched battle at Dien Bien Phu. The plan misfired. Cut off and surrounded, the French were trapped and after 55 days of fierce fighting, they were overrun.

The Liberators

Three of the most remarkable freedom fighters in history refused to accept honours in reward.
● Joan of Arc (1412–1431) was a peasant girl who inspired the French to unite and defeat the English who had seized much of France. She was burned at the stake by her enemies but her spirit lived on to inspire future generations.
● Simon Bolivar (1783–1830), who was known as 'The Liberator' in South America, shunned any other kind of title.
● Giuseppe Garibaldi (1807–1882) led his band of 1000 'redshirts' to free Italy from Austrian rule. When the war was won, and Italy was a united kingdom, Garibaldi retired to the peace and quiet of his farm in the country.

Turning the Tide

─Record Battles─

● **Bloodiest**
First Somme 1916: more than 1,000,000 casualties.

● **Greatest invasion**
D-Day, 6 June 1944: 1,000,000 men landed within four weeks.

● **Longest siege**
Leningrad: 880 days (August 1941 to January 1944).

● **Largest retreat**
Dunkirk, May 1940: 338,000 Allied troops rescued from France.

● **Longest war**
Hundred Years War, 1346–1453: fought between England and France.

● **Shortest war**
Six-Day War, 5-10 June 1967: between Israelis and Arabs.

The Battle of Gettysburg in 1863 was a turning point in the American Civil War. General Robert E. Lee hoped to invade the North, but this bloody battle (in which both sides lost around 23,000 men) left the Confederate army too weak to do more than retreat into the South.

◄ In the summer of 1812, Napoleon marched into Russia with the largest invasion army Europe had yet seen—450,000 men. As the French advanced, the Russians retreated, burning villages and crops as they went. There was only one full-scale battle, Borodino, before the French reached Moscow. They found the city deserted. No word came from the Czar about surrender, and snow began to fall. With no warm winter clothing and with their supplies running low, the French had no choice but to retreat. The long march home was a nightmare. Thousands died from cold and starvation, or were killed by marauding Russian Cossacks. Fewer than 40,000 survivors reached France.

The Battle of Britain

In the summer of 1940 the German Luftwaffe launched an air attack on Britain. By destroying the Royal Air Force, Germany hoped to prepare the way for a full-scale invasion. A new invention, radar, played an important part in Britain's defences as waves of German bombers and fighters attacked southern England. The RAF's Hurricanes and Spitfires shot down many of the enemy planes, and finally forced the Germans to abandon their invasion plans.

The Zulus were the most warlike Africans in southern Africa. Their impis (regiments) terrorized other tribes. In 1879 a Zulu force surprised a British army camp at Isandhlwana in Natal. The British had failed to protect the camp properly and were overrun. After this victory, the Zulus moved on to attack a small post known as Rorke's Drift. No more than eighty fit soldiers manned the post, with some thirty or so sick and wounded men. Nevertheless, with the aid of guns, the tiny garrison fought off the Zulus in fierce hand-to-hand fighting.

Battles of Conquest

▲ Before the Battle of Hastings, the English had marched north to repel an invading army from Norway. They then hurried south at the news that William and his Norman army had landed in Sussex. Harold at once sought battle. The English fought on foot, with axes and spears, but the Normans had brought horses across the Channel. The English 'shield wall' held fast on Senlac Hill until the Normans pretended to retreat. Sensing victory, the English broke ranks and pursued them. When the Normans turned and counter-attacked, many English were killed and the battle swung in William's favour.

Makers

The course of history has sometimes been decided by a single battle. Had the English, and not the Normans, won the Battle of Hastings in 1066, English history might have been very different. Like many important battles, Hastings was lost by a combination of bad tactics and bad luck.

The English king, Harold, made a mistake in rushing into battle too soon. At the height of the battle, the Normans tricked the English into leaving their strong hilltop position. Finally, luck played its part when Harold himself was killed. Without its leader, the English army lost heart and was scattered.

Bold conquerors have often been favoured by fortune. Genghis Khan, Tamerlane and Babur all won empires in the East through victories on the battlefield. But defenders have also been fortunate—as when the English fleet humbled the mighty Armada in 1588.

The Crusades

For 200 years Christians and Moslems fought for possession of the Holy Land (Palestine). In the 11th century the warlike Seljuk Moslems refused to allow Christian pilgrims to go there. Encouraged by the Church, the Christian kings of Europe led a series of expeditions or crusades to take the Holy Land. In all there were seven, but only the first in 1096 was successful. Later the Christians spent more time quarrelling among themselves than fighting the Moslems. In 1187 Saladin recaptured Jerusalem and, although the Crusaders held the stronghold of Acre until 1291, they never again managed to wrest the Holy Land from Moslem rule.

◄ The Moghul Empire, which dominated India for 300 years, was founded by Babur (1483-1530). He was descended from two earlier conquerors, Tamerlane and Genghis Khan. With a tiny army of only 300 tribesmen, the young Babur captured Kabul in Afghanistan in 1504 and invaded India. In 1526 his army fought a great battle at Panipat against the Sultan Ibrahim, who had raised an army four times the size of Babur's. However, Babur had skilled artillery and musketeers, and he positioned his guns behind a barricade of carts. The gunfire terrified Ibrahim's elephants and at the end of the battle 20,000 of his men lay dead.

▲ The Spanish Armada was an invasion fleet of 130 great galleons, packed with troops. For a week, it fought a running battle in the Channel against the English, whose ships were smaller but better armed and faster. When the Armada anchored off Calais, the English sent in fireships to drive it out to sea again. Those Spanish ships that escaped the English guns fled into the North Sea. Many of the survivors were sunk in fierce gales as they tried to sail home round the treacherous coasts of Scotland and Ireland.

▶ Three scenes from the Battle of Blenheim, 1704. Left: English infantry advance across the River Nebel. Centre: A brigade of French foot soldiers, abandoned by their cavalry, are cut down. Right: Prince Eugene's Austrians press home the Allied attack on the French flank. Marlborough's plan of campaign meant risking his entire army by marching from the Netherlands into Southern Germany. His victory over the French and Bavarians at Blenheim saved the Austrian capital, Vienna, and thwarted French ambitions of controlling all Europe.

Struggle for Power

The 'balance of power' has shifted uneasily throughout history, as nations and sometimes religions have struggled for supremacy. In the early Middle Ages, the religion of Islam swept through Arabia. The followers of the prophet Mohammed believed in 'holy war', and this rising tide of Islam brought East and West into conflict—in Spain, in the Holy Land, and in what remained of the old Roman Empire.

The capital of the eastern Roman Empire was Constantinople. When it fell to the Turks in 1453, the long reign of the Byzantine emperors was ended. In Europe religious quarrels caused long and bitter wars, such as the Thirty Years War (1618–1648) in Germany. For many years, too, Catholic Spain and Protestant England were enemies.

The defeat of the Spanish Armada in 1588 saved England from invasion.

The struggle for supremacy in Europe often involved France, particularly during the reign of Louis XIV (1643–1715). He wanted to rule all Europe. During the War of the Spanish Succession, England, Holland and Austria joined forces against France. The Allied commander was the great Duke of Marlborough, who believed the key to victory was attack. Marlborough trained his infantry to fire musket volleys before advancing with bayonets fixed. Cavalry rammed home the attack, charging with swords drawn. With these tactics and Marlborough's bold plan of campaign, the Allies won at Blenheim in 1704 and foiled the French king's ambitions.

The Great War

In August 1914 when the Great War, now known as World War I, began thousands of men rushed to join the armed forces. People sang and cheered as the soldiers marched off to fight. By the end of 1914 this mood had completely changed. Instead of rejoicing, people were shocked, as the war had become a dreadful disaster. Many people thought the war would be over quickly, but it was to last four years.

Both sides had guns so powerful that they could fire shells for hours on end, destroying everything within range. Many battles began with huge artillery 'barrages'. When the guns stopped firing, all that was left was a sea of mud and ruins. A single machine gun could slaughter dozens of men in minutes. Armies could not move forward against such guns, so they dug themselves lines of trenches.

Most of the great battles of this war took place in Europe, where a great line of trenches and barbed wire stretched from the Belgian coast to the Alps, with Germany and its allies on one side, and France, Britain and their allies on the other. Hundreds of thousands of men died in gaining just a few metres of ground for their side.

Tanks were first used in 1916 by the British. The Germans were terrified to see these crawling 'tin boxes' and ran away.

This was the first war in which men fought in the air. Pilots in light, fragile planes fired at each other with pistols and machine guns. They had no parachutes, so could not escape if their planes were shot down.

For the first time, too, people living far from the battlefields were attacked. The Germans flew Zeppelin airships to drop bombs on Britain.

In 1917 the Americans entered the war, and in 1918 the Germans and their allies surrendered. About 10 million soldiers had been killed. Never before had there been such death, destruction and suffering.

◀ After the Battle of Jutland (1916) the German navy did not fight another big sea battle against the British.

During World War I many new machines and kinds of equipment were tested and used in war for the first time. It was the first truly mechanized war.

'Dogfights' in the air

▲ Zeppelin airships flew to Britain and dropped bombs. They frightened people more than causing much destruction.

Gas mask

Ambulance

Barbed wire

Italian Cerrano
75 mm Auto Cannone

British Mk IV
Male 2324 tank

The World at War

On December 7, 1941, nearly 200 Japanese planes, launched from aircraft carriers, made a surprise attack on the US naval base of Pearl Harbor, Hawaii. Three battleships were destroyed and others badly damaged. But the Japanese missed the US carriers, which were at sea. The raid brought the United States into World War II. And it was carriers, not out-of-date battleships, that won the naval battles fought in the Pacific.

Until modern times, most wars were local, hence their names: the Afghan War, the Zulu War, the Ashanti War and so on. Often quite small numbers of fighting men were involved. It is true that wars often lasted many years. For a hundred years in the Middle Ages, England and France were at war. But, generally speaking, ordinary people could manage to stay clear of the battlefields, and life went on more or less normally.

The most bitter war is probably civil war, in which opposing factions within a country fight for power. The English Civil War (1642–1652) is an example. However, this war was nothing like so bloody as the American Civil War (1861–1865). Weapons had become much more deadly and, so desperate were the battles, it was often difficult to decide if either side had really won any kind of victory.

World War I (1914–1918) started in Europe and was mostly fought there, although fighting spread to the Middle East and East Africa. For the first time submarines attacked merchant shipping. This meant that even countries not engaged in the fighting also suffered. For the first time, too, towns and cities were bombed from the air by airships and aeroplanes. So many men were fighting at 'the front', that women took over the production of vital supplies.

World War I was called 'the war to end wars'. But from 1939 to 1945 the world went to war again. In World War II few parts of the globe were far from the fighting. Millions of civilians were killed or became refugees. Armies fought across Europe and in Asia, while the naval war was fought in the Atlantic and Pacific oceans. Machines, notably tanks and aircraft, dominated the fighting. The close of World War II saw the first long range rocket weapons—the German V1 flying bomb and V2 rocket—and, finally, the appalling atom bombs which were dropped on Japan in 1945.

▲ Russian peasants flee from the German advance on Moscow. World War II involved civilians as much as it did soldiers.

▲ Aircraft carriers played an important part in the war at sea.

After more than two years' preparation, Allied soldiers, under the combined command of General Eisenhower, landed on the Normandy beaches on D-Day, 6 June 1944. Within the first week, more than 325,000 men, 50,000 vehicles and 100,000 tonnes of equipment poured into France. But it took almost another year of bitter fighting before the war in Europe came to an end.

Key Dates

Major Battles

GREEKS AND ROMANS

Marathon 490 BC Force of 10,000 Athenians and allies defeated 50,000 Persian troops, crushing a Persian invasion attempt.

Salamis 480 BC Greek fleet of 360 ships defeated Persian fleet of 1000 ships. Persians had to withdraw from Greece.

Siege of Syracuse 414–413 BC Athenians besieged city of Syracuse in the Peloponnesian War; siege ended when night attack led by Athenian general Demosthenes was crushed.

Aegospotami 405 BC Spartan fleet under Lysander defeated last Athenian fleet, and ended the Peloponnesian War.

Arbela 331 BC Alexander the Great's Greek army defeated a Persian force twice the size under Darius III, conquering Persia. The battle was fought at Gaugamela 40 km (25 mi) from Arbela.

Zama 202 BC Romans under Scipio Africanus defeated the Carthaginians under Hannibal, winning Second Punic War.

Actium 31 BC Roman fleet of 400 ships under Octavian (later Emperor Augustus) defeated 500 ships, combined fleet of Mark Antony and Cleopatra. The victory made Octavian master of Rome and its empire.

Teutoberg Forest AD 9 German tribesmen under the chief Arminius destroyed three Roman legions, ending Roman plans to invade and conquer their lands.

Adrianople AD 378 Visigoths under Fridigern defeated and killed the Roman Emperor Valens at Adrianople (now Edirne, Turkey).

Châlons-sur-Marne AD 451 Romans led by Flavius Aetius and Visigoths led by Theodoric I defeated the Huns under Attila.

EARLY EUROPE

Tours 732 The Franks under Charles Martel defeated the Saracens (Muslims), halting their advance in western Europe.

Lech 955 Emperor Otto the Great ended the Magyar threat in western Europe.

Hastings 1066 About 8000 troops under Duke William of Normandy defeated an equal force under Saxon king Harold II. England thereafter came under Norman rule.

Crécy 1346 Invading army of 10,000 English under Edward III defeated 20,000 French. English archers won the day.

▲ **The defeat of the Persian fleet at Salamis in 480 BC forced Xerxes and his army back into Asia.**

Poitiers 1356 Edward the Black Prince of England crushed a French army, capturing the French King John II.

Agincourt 1415 Henry V of England with 10,000 troops defeated 30,000 Frenchmen, and recaptured Normandy.

Siege of Orléans 1428–1429 English troops began siege in October 1428, but in April 1429 Joan of Arc came to the aid of city, and forced the besiegers to withdraw. Victory was a turning point in French campaign to drive the English out of France.

Siege of Constantinople 1453 Ottoman Turkish army of more than 100,000 under Mohammed the Conqueror captured the city, held by 10,000 men led by the last Byzantine emperor, Constantine Paleologus.

WARS OF FAITH & SUCCESSION

Lepanto 1571 Allied Christian fleet of 208 galleys under Don John of Austria defeated Ali Pasha's Turkish fleet of 230 galleys.

Invincible Armada 1588 Spanish invasion fleet led by Duke of Medina Sidonia was defeated by the English under Lord Howard of Effingham.

Naseby 1645 Sir Thomas Fairfax with 14,000 Parliamentary troops defeated Prince Rupert with 10,000 Royalist soldiers, virtually ending Charles I's power.

Boyne 1690 William III of England with 35,000 troops routed his rival, James II, with 21,000 men, ending Stuart hopes of regaining the throne.

Blenheim 1704 A British-Austrian army led by Duke of Marlborough and Prince Eugène defeated the French and Bavarians during the War of the Spanish Succession.

Poltava 1709 The Russians under Peter the Great routed an invading Swedish army led by Charles XII of Sweden, overturning Swedish power in the Baltic.

COLONIAL STRUGGLES

Plassey 1757 Robert Clive with an Anglo-Indian army of 3000 defeated the Nawab of Bengal's army of 60,000, conquering Bengal and setting Britain on the road to domination in India.

Quebec 1759 British troops under James Wolfe made a night attack up the St Lawrence River, climbing the cliffs to the Plains of Abraham overlooking the city. They defeated the French forces under the Marquis de Montcalm; he and Wolfe were killed.

Saratoga 1777 British troops under John Burgoyne surrendered to American colonial forces under Horatio Gates; defeat led France to declare war on Britain.

Yorktown 1781 Charles Cornwallis with 8000 British troops was bottled in, and surrendered to a larger force under George Washington, ending the American War of Indepedence.

AGE OF NAPOLEON

Valmy 1792 A French Revolutionary army defeated the Prussians in heavy fog. The victory gave new heart to the Revolutionary forces in France.

Nile 1798 Horatio Nelson commanding a British fleet of 15 ships destroyed a 16-ship French fleet under Francis Paul Brueys in Aboukïr Bay, cutting off Napoleon Bonaparte's French army in Egypt.

▼ **The Battle of Lepanto, in 1571. A Turkish fleet of about 300 ships clashed with a smaller Christian fleet. The two fleets fought in rigid formations. Ships closed with one another and the soldiers on board engaged in hand-to-hand combat.**

Trafalgar 1805 British fleet of 27 ships under Horatio Nelson shattered Franco-Spanish fleet of 33 ships under Pierre de Villeneuve, ending Napoleon's hopes of invading England. Nelson was killed.

Austerlitz 1805 Emperor Napoleon I with 65,000 French troops defeated an 83,000-strong Austro-Russian army under the Austrian and Russian emperors. The Austrians sued for peace, and the Russians withdrew. Called *Battle of the Three Emperors.*

Jena and Auerstädt 1806 French forces routed the main Prussian armies on the same day (October 14), shattering Prussian power.

Leipzig 1813 Napoleon I with 190,000 French troops was surrounded and crushed by an allied force of 300,000 Austrian, Prussian, Russian and Swedish troops. This *Battle of the Nations* ended Napoleon's domination of Europe.

Waterloo 1815 A British, Dutch, and Belgian force of 67,000 fought off 74,000 French troops under Napoleon I until the arrival of the Prussian army of Gebhard von Blücher. It ended Napoleon's final bid for power.

FIRST MODERN CONFLICTS

Gettysburg 1863 Federal forces under George Meade defeated Robert E. Lee's Confederate army, a turning point in the American Civil War.

Vicksburg 1863 Federal general Ulysses S. Grant captured Confederate army under John Pemberton, the day after Gettysberg.

Sedan 1870 French army of 100,000 men defeated and surrounded by German force of more than twice the size in decisive battle of Franco-Prussian War.

Tsushima 1905 Japanese fleet destroyed Russian fleet of equal size, bringing victory for Japan in Russo-Japanese War.

WORLD WAR I

Marne 1914 French and British armies halted German forces invading France. From then on war on the Western Front became a trench-based slogging match.

First battle of Ypres 1914 German forces trying to reach Calais lost 150,000 men; British and French armies held off attack, losing more than 100,000 men.

Verdun 1916 In a six-month struggle French forces held off a major attack by German armies commanded by Crown Prince William. French losses were 348,000 men, the German losses 328,000.

Jutland 1916 British Grand Fleet led by John Jellicoe fought German High Seas Fleet under Rheinhard Scheer. The Germans never again ventured out to sea.

Somme 1916 In a 141-day battle following Verdun British and French captured 320 sq km (125 sq mi) of ground, losing 600,000 men; German defenders lost almost 500,000.

Passchendaele 1917 (also known as third battle of Ypres). British forces launched eight attacks over 102 days in heavy rain and through thick mud, gaining 8 km (5 miles) and losing 400,000 men.

St Mihiel Salient 1918 American victory in World War I: German line broken and Salient flattened out. In first major air battle 1480 Allied planes defeated German air force.

▲ **General Joffre, who, with great calm, held together his army on the Marne in the face of disaster and with brilliant timing seized the opportunity he needed to thwart the German advance.**

▲ **General Robert E. Lee, soldier and gentleman, refused an offer of high command in the Union Army to follow his native state of Virginia into the Confederacy. Lee's greatest military talents lay in his tactics on the battlefield. Despite his inferior forces he inflicted several crushing defeats on the Northern armies before the battle of Gettysburg in 1863.**

▶ Captured German troops in tattered uniforms march in the bitter cold near the ruins of Stalingrad.

▶ Far right: General Bernard Montgomery, Commander of the Eighth Army, keeps an eye on the progress of the battle of Alamein from a Grant tank.

WORLD WAR II

Britain 1940 A German air force of 2500 planes launched an attack lasting 114 days to try to win air supremacy over Britain. The smaller Royal Air Force defeated the attack, preventing a German invasion.
Coral Sea 1942 American fleet drove back a Japanese invasion fleet bound for New Guinea in four-day battle in which all the fighting was done by aeroplanes.
Midway 1942 A 100-ship Japanese fleet led by Isoruko Yamamoto aiming to capture Midway Island was defeated by American fleet half the size, under Raymond Spruance.
El Alamein 1942 British Eighth Army under Bernard Montgomery drove back German Afrika Korps under Erwin Rommel, out of Egypt and deep into Libya.
Stalingrad 1942–1943 Twenty-one German divisions tried to capture Stalingrad (now Volgograd), but siege was broken, and Friedrich von Paulus had to surrender with more than 100,000 German troops.
Normandy 1944 Allied forces under Dwight D. Eisenhower invaded German-held northern France in biggest-ever sea-borne attack; after a month of heavy fighting Normandy was cleared and Germans began to retreat.
Leyte Gulf 1944 US 3rd and 7th fleets defeated a Japanese force, ending Japanese naval power in World War II.
Ardennes Bulge 1944–1945 Last German counter-attack in west through Ardennes Forest failed; Germans lost 100,000 casualties and 110,000 prisoners.

POST-WAR

Inchon 1950 US forces made surprise landing behind North Korean lines in Korean War, leading to major victory over North Korea.
Dien Bien Phu 1954 French surrendered to Vietminh after 8-week siege; end of French influence in Indochina.

▶ A French paratroop battalion counter-attacks during the battle of Dien Bien Phu.

Major Wars

Persian spearman
500 BC

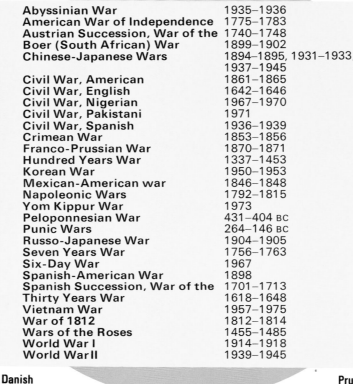

English archer
1350

Abyssinian War	1935–1936
American War of Independence	1775–1783
Austrian Succession, War of the	1740–1748
Boer (South African) War	1899–1902
Chinese-Japanese Wars	1894–1895, 1931–1933, 1937–1945
Civil War, American	1861–1865
Civil War, English	1642–1646
Civil War, Nigerian	1967–1970
Civil War, Pakistani	1971
Civil War, Spanish	1936–1939
Crimean War	1853–1856
Franco-Prussian War	1870–1871
Hundred Years War	1337–1453
Korean War	1950–1953
Mexican-American war	1846–1848
Napoleonic Wars	1792–1815
Yom Kippur War	1973
Peloponnesian War	431–404 BC
Punic Wars	264–146 BC
Russo-Japanese War	1904–1905
Seven Years War	1756–1763
Six-Day War	1967
Spanish-American War	1898
Spanish Succession, War of the	1701–1713
Thirty Years War	1618–1648
Vietnam War	1957–1975
War of 1812	1812–1814
Wars of the Roses	1455–1485
World War I	1914–1918
World War II	1939–1945

Danish
guardsman
1640

Prussian
foot soldier
1750

FOOT SOLDIERS THROUGH THE AGES

Russian
soldier
1812

Confederate,
US Civil War
1863

US infantryman
1942

German machine-
gunner 1914

Index

Acknowledgements

Photographs: 6 Victoria and Albert Museum; 7 Mary Evans; 9 Imperial War Museum *top,* Science Museum *centre;* Associated Press *bottom;* 10 Scala; 12 Musée de la Ville de Strasbourg *top,* Mansell *bottom;* 12/13 Bibliothèque Nationale, 13 National Portrait Gallery; 23 Mansell, *top,* National Army Museum *bottom;* 18 Radio Times Hulton Picture Library *top* and *centre,* Mary Evans *bottom;* 19 Imperial War Museum; 21 Bodleian Library; 23 Paris Match; 24 Bulloz Musée de l'Armee *top,* Gettysburg National Military Park *bottom;* 29 National Army Museum; 33 Novosti *top,* Imperial War Museum *centre;* 34 Mary Evans Picture Library; 35 National Maritime Museum; 36 Mary Evans Picture Library *left,* Popperfoto *right;* 37 Imperial War Museum *top right,* John Hillelson Agency *bottom.*

Picture research: Penny Warn.

ST. EDMUNDS COLLEGE
205 Prinsep Street
Collie W.A. 6225